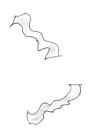

# It's
# Raining
# Pigs &
# Noodles

drawings by
# JAMES STEVENSON

poems by

# JACK PRELUTSKY

# IT'S RAINING PIGS & NOODLES

**GREENWILLOW BOOKS**
*An Imprint of HarperCollinsPublishers*

Library of Congress Cataloging-in-Publication Data

Prelutsky, Jack.
It's raining pigs & noodles / poems by Jack Prelutsky;
drawings by James Stevenson.
    p. cm.
"Greenwillow Books."
Summary: A collection of humorous poems such as
"The Dancing Hippopotami," "You Can't Make Me Eat That,"
"My Father's Name is Sasquatch," and "Dear Wumbledeedumble."
ISBN 0-06-029194-X (trade).    ISBN 0-06-029195-8 (lib. bdg.)
1. Children's poetry, American.    [1. Humorous poetry.
2. American poetry.]    I. Title: It's raining pigs & noodles.
II. Stevenson, James, (date) ill.    III. Title.
PS3566.R36I828 2000    811'.54—dc21    00-024707

1 2 3 4 5 6 7 8 9 10    First Edition

In memory of Manoa Jojola

## It's Raining Pigs and Noodles

It's raining pigs and noodles,
it's pouring frogs and hats,
chrysanthemums and poodles,
bananas, brooms, and cats.
Assorted prunes and parrots
are dropping from the sky,
here comes a bunch of carrots,
some hippopotami.

It's raining pens and pickles,
and eggs and silverware.
A flood of figs and nickels
is falling through the air.
I see a swan, a sweater,
a clock, a model train—
I like this so much better
than when it's raining rain.

## My Underdog Is Overweight

My underdog is overweight,
he has an underbite,
he tends to tunnel underground
and stay there overnight.

That overactive underdog
is often hard to bear . . .
he overate my overcoat
and all my underwear.

## The Chicken Club

We are members in good standing
of **THE CHICKEN CLUB**, and yes,
we confess we all are chicken,
though you probably could guess.
We are frightened of our shadows,
of our own reflections too,
and we shriek and run for cover
when we hear a sudden "Boo!"

We are terrified of thunder,
and we scramble at the sound.
We are scared of tiny creatures
in the air and on the ground.
We are jittery and jumpy,
so afraid of many things,
that we've even started clucking,
and we're sprouting chicken wings.

### Noisy, Noisy

It's noisy, noisy overhead,
the birds are winging south,
and every bird is opening
a noisy, noisy mouth.

They fill the air with loud complaint,
they honk and quack and squawk—
they do not feel like flying,
but it's much too far to walk.

## The Bunny Bus

All aboard the *Bunny Bus*,
pay your fares, and do not fuss.
You will find your ride ideal,
there's a hare behind the wheel.

Passengers, please keep your seats
as we speed along the streets.
When you're going anywhere,
*Rabbit Transit* gets you there.

## I Chased a Dragon Through the Woods

I chased a dragon through the woods,
haranguing him all day.
"I'll catch you soon!" I taunted.
"You can never get away.
There's no escaping me, my friend,"
I confidently cried.
"You might as well stop running,
there is nowhere you can hide.

"I think that I will simply lop
your head off with my sword."
The dragon stopped and whirled about
and ominously roared.

**"You'd better think again,"** he boomed,
 and glared into my eyes.
**"In case you hadn't noticed,
 I'm a dozen times your size.
 It's evident that I'd prevail
 if ever we should fight,
 I'm quite accomplished with my claws,
 and furthermore, I bite!"**

I thought about the dragon's words,
and couldn't disagree—
I chased a dragon through the woods,
and now he's chasing me.

## My First Best Friend

My first best friend is Awful Ann—
she socked me in the eye.
My second best is Sneaky Sam—
he tried to swipe my pie.
My third best friend is Max the Rat—
he trampled on my toes.
My fourth best friend is Nasty Nell—
she almost broke my nose.

My fifth best friend is Ted the Toad—
he kicked me in the knee.
My sixth best friend is Grumpy Gail—
she's always mean to me.
My seventh best is Monster Moe—
he often plays too rough.
That's all the friends I've got right now—
I think I've got enough.

## See What Happened!

See what happened! Hapless Peter
turned into a parking meter.
On the curb he stands all day,
wishing dogs would go away.

## <u>My Parents Have the Flu Today</u>

My parents have the flu today,
they both are sick in bed,
and thoughts of things to do today
are swimming through my head.
My nimble brain is burgeoning
with ways to misbehave,
I'll give my brother's Teddy Bear
a haircut and a shave.

Perhaps I'll make a mud pie
in my sister's stupid hat,
attach my mother's earrings
to the puppy and the cat,
hang carrots from the ceiling,
stuff bananas into shoes,
then set the clocks to different times,
it's certain to confuse.

I'll switch the salt and sugar,
scatter meatballs on the rugs,
hide spaghetti in a closet,
and refrigerate some bugs.
I'll paint my father's underwear
an iridescent blue.
My options are unlimited . . .
my parents have the flu.

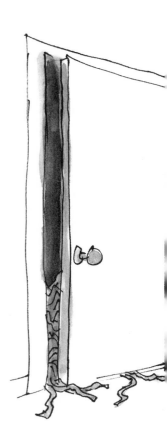

### I Awakened with a Feeling

I awakened with a feeling
that was not exactly fright,
after something ate the feathers
in my pillow overnight.

### The Loco Boys

The Loco Boys were rustlers
who rode the western plains.
A pack of mangy outlaws,
they came up short on brains.

The ranchers plain ignored them,
no posse chased those thieves.
They never rustled cattle—
they only rustled leaves.

## The Time Has Come

I think the time has come to throw
the jack-o'-lantern out,
it smells less like a pumpkin
than it does like sauerkraut.
Its expression is peculiar,
it has lost its friendly grin,
it's tilting sort of strangely,
and its cheeks are caving in.

Its forehead is collapsing,
and its eyes are heading south,
its nose is now connected
to the middle of its mouth.
I admit it's been the focus
of some happy family scenes,
but we've had that jack-o'-lantern
for eleven Halloweens.

# I'm Sitting Underneath a Chair

I'm sitting underneath a chair,
the chair is overturned,
though if in fact it weren't there,
I wouldn't be concerned.
I understand most people try
to sit upon a seat,
but I prefer the floor, where I
can look at lots of feet.

I truly do not have a clue
explaining why I choose
to settle down the way I do
and study socks and shoes.
I only stay here for a time,
then off again I crawl
into a corner, where I climb
and perch upon the wall.

## I Ate a Tooth This Morning

I ate a tooth this morning,
it was an accident.
It popped into my cereal,
and bingo, down it went.
Before I started breakfast,
that tooth was in my head,
but now that I have swallowed it,
it's somewhere else instead.

It mingled with some raisins,
and landed deep inside.
Perhaps I might have stopped it . . .
I never even tried.
I'm sorry that it happened,
and sorrier to say
that I will never see again
that tooth I ate today.

## Chocolate-Covered Salami

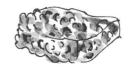

Chocolate-covered salami,
broccoli chocolate fudge,
spinach in chocolate syrup,
chocolate sauerkraut sludge.

Pickles in chocolate pudding,
chocolate fish fricassee—
if it has chocolate on it,
it is a snack made for me.

## The Dancing Hippopotami

The Dancing Hippopotami,
in opulent array,
performed with great agility
an intricate ballet.

The Dancing Hippopotami
then flew into a rage,
for on their final pirouette,
they crashed right through the stage.

## The Sniffing Snutterwudds

We are the Sniffing Snutterwudds,
we have a dozen noses,
half of them are tiny buds,
and half are almost hoses.

We love the scent of roses,
and we sniff them through and through,
but we shut down our noses
when a skunk comes into view.

## My Sister Shrieked, Astonished

My sister shrieked, astonished, and my brother ducked his head. A pigeon lost a feather, an unset etter fled. The mailman dropped his letters, and a cat leapt in the air — when next I throw my boomerang, I'll exercise more care.

## I Built a Fabulous Machine

I built a fabulous machine
to keep my room completely clean.
It swept it up in nothing flat—
has anybody seen the cat?

## My Sister Whispered Magic Words

My sister whispered magic words
directly in my ear,
The second that she said them
I began to disappear.
She said her words a second time,
I couldn't even think,
for suddenly I wasn't there,
I'd vanished in a blink.

I haven't got the least idea
where I am standing now,
I'd like to get back home again,
but simply don't know how.
I hope this doesn't last too long,
for though it doesn't hurt,
my mother's making chocolate cake . . .
I hate to miss dessert.

## Her Highness Zookeepoo

I am Her Highness Zookeepoo,
and what I say, you've got to do.
Pay close attention, beasts and birds,
and act at once upon my words.
I hereby issue royal decrees
commanding kangaroos to sneeze,
directing shrews to play charades
and sheep to dress in window shades.

From this day forward, swans and skunks
must be togged in bathing trunks,
porcupines must sing duets,
camels must play castanets.
Newts must henceforth tootle flutes,
bears must carry bumbershoots,
ducks must juggle, geese must dance,
mice must tickle elephants.

Parrots must play tag with cats,
beavers must wear bowler hats,
rats must learn to roller skate,
bats must be in bed by eight.
Although you may not like my laws,
you must obey them all, because
I am Her Highness Zookeepoo,
and what I say, you've got to do.

### Grungy Grace

I am extremely devious,
my name is Grungy Grace.
I hardly ever brush my teeth
or wash my hands and face.
"It's time to wash," my father says,
but since I'm not a dope,
I simply turn the water on
and wet the towel and soap.

"Brush your teeth," my mother says,
I never even blink.
I squeeze out gobs of toothpaste,
and I brush the bathroom sink.
I'm very good at fooling them,
my brain's extremely keen,
but I've got lots of rashes,
and my teeth are turning green.

## Never Never Disagree

Never never disagree
with a shark beneath the sea,
lest you feel a sudden crunch
and discover you are lunch.

## Hiccup!

I have *hiccup* hiccup hiccups,

I've had hiccup them all day.

They're persistent hiccup hiccup

and won't hiccup go away.

I've tried gulping hiccup water,

stood upon my hiccup head,

held my breath until my hiccup

hiccup face turned hiccup red.

I've attempted every hiccup

hiccup hiccup cure I could,

but it hasn't hiccup hiccup

done a hiccup bit of good.

And in fact I think I'm hiccup

getting hiccup hiccup worse.

Do I need a hiccup doctor

or a *hiccup* hiccup nurse?

I can feel my hiccup hiccups

down into my hiccup shoes.

I have hiccup got the hiccup

hiccup hiccup hiccup blues.

I'm afraid my hiccup insides

are about to hiccup pop,

if these hiccup hiccups hiccup

do not hiccup hiccup stop.

## A Famous Monster

I am a famous monster
who roams from place to place,
renowned by reputation,
though few have seen my face.
My arms and legs are scrawny,
my torso is the same,
my hands are both gigantic,
they're how I've gained my fame.

Unlike my raucous colleagues,
who fill the air with roars,
I'm not by nature noisy,
until I knock on doors.
One knock is quite sufficient
to make a door collapse—
I'm called **THE KNOCK-LESS MONSTER**.
Do I exist? Perhaps!

## Tomorrow's My Unbirthday

Tomorrow's my unbirthday,
and I can hardly wait,
for every day I have one
is a day to celebrate.
I love unbirthday parties,
my friends enjoy them too,
we love to play unbirthday games . . .
I always win a few.

I love unbirthday presents,
they fill me with delight,
I love my grand unbirthday cakes
and savor every bite.
Tomorrow's my unbirthday,
I'm overjoyed, hooray!
I also had one yesterday,
I'm having one today.

## Quibble Q. Quing

I'm Quibble Q. Quing,
and I think about things,
I think of why elephants
do not need wings,
why oceans are salty,
and mountains are high,
why chickens have feathers,
and foxes are sly.

I sit and I wonder,
I ponder and muse
why hands fit in mittens,
and feet fit in shoes,
why rings form a circle,
and marbles are round,
why when you are silent,
you don't make a sound.

I think and I think
and I try to explain
why winks happen quickly,
why links make a chain,
why lemons are yellow,
and spinach is green,
and why the invisible
cannot be seen.

I often reflect
on why horses have hair,
why fishes need water,
and airplanes need air,
why hammers have handles,
and banjos have strings . . .
I'm Quibble Q. Quing,
and I think about things.

## It's Awkward

It's awkward being taller
than the average giraffe,
to cram into a room
I have to fold myself in half.
Although I'm rather flexible,
it's nonetheless a chore
when my rear is near the ceiling
and my ears are near the floor.

When I am out in public,
and you'd like to talk to me,
unless you've got a ladder,
you should climb the nearest tree.
This tends to be impractical,
so people rarely try
to rise up to my altitude
and see me eye to eye.

As I stroll down the avenue,
I'm something of a sight,
people often point at me,
they wonder at my height.
Many gawk and even gasp,
a few are apt to laugh.
It's awkward being taller
than the average giraffe.

## A Princess Laments

I kissed a frog because I'd heard
that it would turn into a prince.
That's not exactly what occurred,
and I've been croaking ever since.

## You Can't Make Me Eat That

You can't make me eat that,
it's slimy and gooey
and icky and yucky
and greasy and gluey.
It looks like you made it
from maggots and mud,
some chopped hippopotamus,
bug heads and blood.

I hate it, I hate it,
I hate it to bits!
Just thinking about it
is giving me fits.
One taste and I'm certain
I'll instantly die . . .
You can't make me eat that,
so don't even try.

# I'm Raising a Virtual Chicken

I'm raising a virtual chicken,
the best of her virtual brood,
I'm serving her virtual water,
I'm feeding her virtual food.
I'm giving her all the attention
a virtual chicken could need,
determined my virtual chicken
will flourish and fully succeed.

My virtual chicken was thriving
and having a wonderful time,
the star of her virtual hen house,
a bird in her virtual prime.
But lately my virtual chicken
appears to have virtual stress,
it takes me a virtual hour
to clean up her virtual mess.

She's under the virtual weather,
her virtual vision is weak,
she can't fluff a virtual feather
or open her virtual beak.
My virtual chicken is ailing,
she staggers on virtual legs,
my virtual chicken is failing
to lay any virtual eggs.

I'm doing my best to revive her,
with round-the-clock virtual care.
Despite all my virtual efforts,
she hasn't a virtual prayer.
I fear that my virtual chicken
has run out of virtual luck.
Farewell, ancient virtual chicken—
hello, baby virtual duck.

## A Greedy and Ambitious Cow

A greedy and ambitious cow
determined she would graze
on all the fields for miles around . . .
she grazed for days and days.

She finished every blade of grass,
the land is barren now.
That cow was in a meadow—
the meadow's in that cow.

### The World's Fastest Turtle

The world's fastest turtle
and world's slowest horse
raced one another
around a great course.

The horse won the race,
you'd expect that, of course . . .
a turtle's a turtle,
a horse is a horse.

### Percy's Perfect Pies

I am Percival P. Puffinwuff,
a baker of renown,
justly famous for creating
the most tasty pies in town.
I make pies for all occasions,
many flavors, any size,
here's a savory assortment
served at **Percy's Perfect Pies**.

**PUMPKIN PANDA CORIANDER**

**CASSOWARY CURDLED CREAM**

**SALSA SALMON SALAMANDER**

SKUNK ASPARAGUS SUPREME

*MANGO KANGAROO VANILLA*

MINNOW MARROW MARZIPAN

**CHICKEN CHICKADEE CHINCHILLA**

**GNU MERINGUE ORANGUTAN**

GOUDA GUPPY GOPHER GRISTLE

**APPLE CAPPUCCINO RAT**

SUSHI GOULASH THRUSH AND THISTLE

PHILODENDRON FERRET FAT

*WEEVIL JELLY VERMICELLI*

WASP IN WALNUT WALRUS SAUCE

BOYSENBERRY BISON BELLY

MACARONI MELON MOSS

MARINARA BAT BANANA

ALLIGATOR BEES AND CHEESE

TAFFY TARRAGON IGUANA

TETRAZZINI ZEBRA KNEES

PRUNE PAPAYA POPPY PARROT

POSSUM PENGUIN PRICKLY PEAR

**CATERPILLAR COLA CARROT**

GORGONZOLA POLAR BEAR

I cannot imagine anything
more wonderful than these,
filled with succulent ingredients
and guaranteed to please.
Every one is so delicious,
it deserves to win a prize
for the principal proprietor
of **Percy's Perfect Pies**.

## I Know I Have a Pointy Head

I know I have a pointy head,
and that I'm long and narrow.
But still, that archer had no right
to use me as an arrow.

## The Otter and the Ocelot

The otter and the ocelot,
as fortunate as they could be,
now sail the seas upon their yacht—
they won the OCELOTTERY.

### A Bicycle Spoke

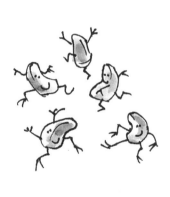

A bicycle spoke,
and a clock stopped to hear.
The tulip blew kisses,
the rose shed a tear.
A package was rapt,
though the shoes weren't swayed,
the cashews went crazy,
a knot was afraid.

The buttons were frightened,
the butter stood pat,
as socks offered punch
to a top in a hat.
A cake pounded hard
when a lock sang off-key,
a plum bobbed a bit,
which the saw didn't see.

The chair took the floor,
for the knight wouldn't stand,
the benches were bored
when the iron was banned.
The tires grew weary,
the forks hit the hay,
the trees left the scene,
as the cheese led the way.

## I Took a Sip of Water

I took a sip of water,
a second sip, a cup.
I filled a tumbler to the brim
and drank that glass right up.
I guzzled down a gallon,
a gallon is a lot,
but noticed that the more I drank,
the thirstier I got.

I drank a quart of lemonade,
I drank a quart of juice,
I drank a quart of chocolate milk,
it wasn't any use.
I found a dozen sodas
and quickly drank them all,
I felt that I could drink a creek,
a lake, a waterfall.

My body kept expanding,
it seemed about to burst,
and yet I couldn't manage
to satisfy my thirst.
Now I've become so bloated,
I can't fit through the door—
I'm fairly certain I will not
eat sponges anymore.

## The Outer Space Miracle Mall

I'm here at **THE OUTER SPACE MIRACLE MALL**,
right at the galaxy's rim.
I'm hunting for bargains I don't need at all
and snapping them up on a whim.
I'm purchasing merchandise scarce in most shops,
like oil that turns gold into cheese,
a gross and a half of invisible mops,
a chair stuffed with overcooked peas.

I found an aquarium riddled with holes,
a penguin that smells like a skunk,
a pair of carnivorous polka-dot moles,
an elephant missing a trunk,
a gadget for putting a cloud in a box,
an oven for baking a star,
a key guaranteed not to fit any locks,
a radioactive guitar.

I'm buying a two-seater woolen canoe,
some cereal made out of sand,
a lifetime supply of inedible stew,
a million-mile-long rubber band,
a wristwatch the size of a medium whale,
a ten-thousand-pound bowling ball . . .
I always enjoy the post-holiday sale
at **THE OUTER SPACE MIRACLE MALL.**

## I Am a Noted Liar

I am a noted liar,
I cannot help but lie.
I never ever tell the truth,
I never even try.
If I say light, it's heavy,
if I say black, it's white,
if I direct you to the left,
you'd best be going right.

I lie about the temperature,
the time and place and date.
No matter what I talk about,
I must prevaricate.
The more and more I practice,
the greater grows my skill.
Don't think that I won't lie to you,
because I surely will.

I weave fantastic stories
and never blink an eye,
it simply is my nature
to lie and lie and lie.
I like to lie a little,
I love to lie a lot,
I'm truly lying to you now,
though honestly, I'm not.

## We're Perched Upon a Star

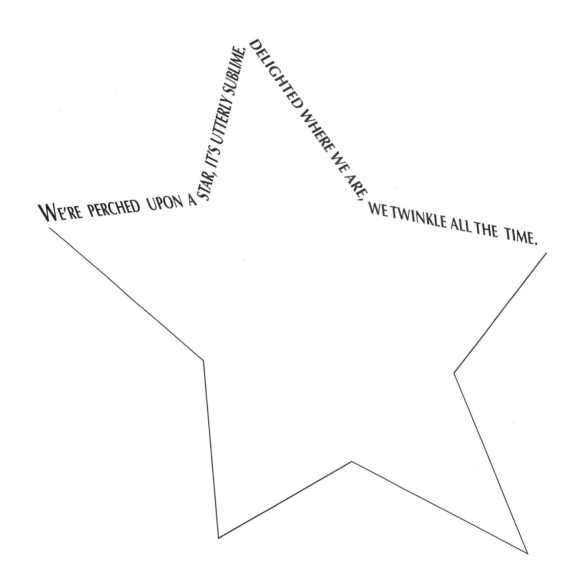

WE'RE PERCHED UPON A STAR, IT'S UTTERLY SUBLIME, DELIGHTED WHERE WE ARE, WE TWINKLE ALL THE TIME.

### What Oinks?

What oinks, is ten feet tall and pink,
and wears a dozen kilts?
It's simple, if you stop and think—
twelve Scottish pigs on stilts.

## Deep in Our Refrigerator

Deep in our refrigerator,
there's a special place
for food that's been around awhile . . .
we keep it, just in case.
"It's probably too old to eat,"
my mother likes to say.
"But I don't think it's old enough
for me to throw away."

It stays there for a month or more
to ripen in the cold,
and soon we notice fuzzy clumps
of multicolored mold.
The clumps are larger every day,
we notice this as well,
but mostly what we notice
is a certain special smell.

When finally it all becomes
a nasty mass of slime,
my mother takes it out, and says,
"Apparently, it's time."
She dumps it in the garbage can,
though not without regret,
then fills that space with other food
that's not so ancient yet.

# I'm Caught Up in Infinity

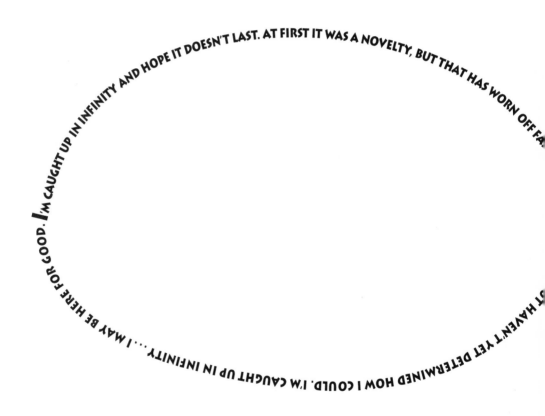

I'M CAUGHT UP IN INFINITY AND HOPE IT DOESN'T LAST. AT FIRST IT WAS A NOVELTY, BUT THAT HAS WORN OFF FA[...]T HAVEN'T YET DETERMINED HOW I COULD. I'M CAUGHT UP IN INFINITY... I MAY BE HERE FOR GOOD.

HAVE PASSED BEFORE AT EVERY TWIST AND BEND. INFINITY, IT'S CLEAR TO ME, DOES NOT BEGIN OR END. IT'S BORING IN INFINITY, THERE'S NO RELIEF IN SIGHT. IT DOESN'T SEEM TO MATTER IF I'M GOING LEFT OR RIGHT. I'D L...

65

# I'm Roaring like a Lion

I'm roaring like a lion,
I'm croaking like a frog,
I'm shrieking like a monkey,
I'm grunting like a hog.

I'm snorting like a buffalo,
I'm whooping like a crane.
My mother's making liver . . .
I thought I should complain.

### Titanic Timmy Tinkletunes

Titanic Timmy Tinkletunes
is such a giant fellow
that when he plays the violin,
he has to use a cello.

## The Sun Is Sinking in the Sky

The sun is sinking in the sky,
I've almost lost the light.
I'd have a bite to eat, but I
have lost my appetite.
I do not know where I am now,
for I have lost my way,
and cannot tell what time it is,
I lost my watch today.

I'd like to build a shelter,
but I've lost my building blocks.
The path is getting rocky,
and I've lost my shoes and socks.
I wish that it were warmer here,
I've lost my shirt and suit.
I'd play a cheery melody,
but I have lost my flute.

I'd stop and sniff the flowers,
but I've lost my sense of smell.
I'm quite unable to cry out,
I've lost my voice as well.
I'm glad I am not hungry,
for I've lost my cheese and bread . . .
I simply don't know what to think,
for I have lost my head.

### The Gummies Are Coming

The Gummies are coming,
be worried, beware!
They're coming to gum up
your fingers and hair.
They're coming on scooters,
they're coming on skates,
with gum on their ladles
and gum on their plates.

The Gummies are coming,
they're coming in force,
by bicycle, tricycle,
tractor, and horse.
Unless you're on guard,
with an excellent plan,
those Gummies will gum you
as much as they can.

The moment they catch you,
they'll gum up your clothes,
your neck and your shoulders,
your ears and your nose.
They'll sneak up behind you,
they never play fair . . .
The Gummies are coming,
be worried, beware!

# My Mother Gave Me Candy

My mother gave me candy . . .
it squirted in my eye.
My sister gave me handkerchiefs . . .
they made me itch and cry.

My father gave me boxing gloves . . .
I touched them and they burst.
Why ever does my birthday
have to fall on April first?

## Butterflies, You Puzzle Me

Butterflies, you puzzle me,
for as you flit and flutter,
I study you, but never see
the slightest bit of butter.

## Chillotta Lott

Chillotta Lott was never warm,
no matter what she wore,
she'd put on seven sweaters
and be colder than before.
In the middle of the summer,
on a day extremely hot,
everyone was sweltering
except Chillotta Lott.

The temperature was ninety nine,
the sun blazed overhead,
her teeth began to chatter,
and her nose glowed cherry red.
The thermometer kept rising,
soon it was one hundred two,
her knees would not stop knocking,
and her face was icy blue.

She added scarves and coats and hats,
she wrapped herself in fur,
but nothing that Chillotta did
was any help to her.
She slipped on extra mittens
at one hundred twelve degrees,
yet started sprouting icicles
and seemed about to freeze.

The temperature grew hotter.
At one hundred twenty five,
she turned so pale that it was clear
she could not long survive.
Chillotta Lott froze solid
at one hundred twenty eight—
she's now a statue in the park
and guards the entrance gate.

## **<u>Purple Orangutans</u>**

Purple orangutans hurtle through space,
silvery unicorns gallop in place,
onions run races with noodles and spoons,
monkeys emerge from enormous cocoons.

Turtles wear sweaters, and pickles wear wigs,
talking tomatoes give lectures to pigs,
peanut-size elephants flutter their wings,
cantaloupes dance as a pineapple sings.

Bison ride bicycles, tigers fly kites,
pelicans flicker their myriad lights,
feathery fishes float high in the air,
radishes wash their luxurious hair.

Rabbits and parrots play tag in the stars,
marshmallows march in the meadows of Mars . . .
these are a few of the wonders I find
in the magic museum I keep in my mind.

## My Father's Name Is Sasquatch

My father's name is Sasquatch,
my mother's name is Yeti.
They often feast on frozen fish,
but I prefer spaghetti.

## I Walk My Dog at Daybreak

I walk my dog at daybreak,
and again right after school.
It's often inconvenient,
but I'm sticking to the rule.
I feed the fish and parakeets,
my hungry cats as well,
then tidy up the litter box
before it starts to smell.

I tend to all the rabbits,
turtles, gerbils, frog, and snake,
and clean the little messes
they inevitably make.
The finches' cage needs freshening,
especially the tray,
and then there are the elephants—
I'm giving them away.

FREE
ELEPHANTS

## The Yaks Convened a Meeting

The yaks convened a meeting,
and a turkey gave a talk,
a cuckoo read the minutes,
and a blue jay took a walk.
A worm perused a novel,
and a penguin took a poll,
a tiger read the news
to an appreciative mole.

The cardinals wore numbers,
and the eagles wore toupees,
the owls were dressed in armor,
and the dogs were in a daze.
The cheetahs brought their chisels,
and the horses brought their saws,
a grouse began complaining
when the crows gave up their cause.

The pigs prepared a picnic,
and the puffins brought canteens,
a beetle snapped a picture
when a pigeon spilled the beans.
The kangaroos all courted,
and the bears gave friendly hugs,
the ducks avoided contact,
and the rats sat on their rugs.

The bats were playing baseball,
and the cats were on the phone,
a lion climbed a mountain,
and a wolf took out a loan.
A bison tried to hover
as a robin stood around,
a wildebeest did nothing,
and a woodchuck hugged the ground.

The swallows finished eating,
and the swans began to sing,
the seals expressed approval,
and the hens jumped in the spring.
A panda raised a ruckus
when a rooster dropped his comb,
the terns reversed direction,
and the hares went marching home.

# The Apathetic Thwo

I am the Apathetic Thwo,
there's nowhere that I want to go,
there's nothing that I want to do,
I have a dreary point of view.
I don't look left, I don't look right,
I don't care if it's dark or light,
I don't look up, I don't look down,
I don't know if I smile or frown.

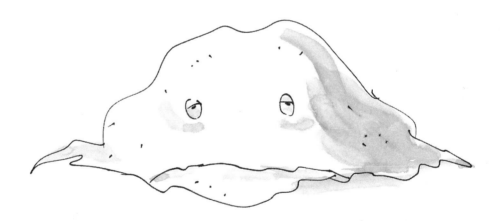

I've not the slightest interest
in north or south, in east or west,
my thoughts are tedious and dull,
my life is at a constant lull.
I do not even seem to care
if I am here, if I am there,
and if my mind were not so small,
I'd wonder why I am at all.

I am the Apathetic Thwo,
oblivious to all I know,
insensitive to all I see,
so nothing much means much to me.
Dispassionate, devoid of cheer,
I never notice what I hear,
and since I'm out of things to say,
you might as well just go away.

## I'm Tortured by Insomnia

I'm tortured by insomnia,
I cannot sleep tonight,
the slightest sound seems louder
than exploding dynamite.
I hear creaking in the kitchen,
I hear squeaking on the stairs,
and the furnace sounds like oxen
being chased by angry bears.

There's a faucet drip-drip-dripping.
roaring like a waterfall,
and outside my bedroom window
I hear ogres playing ball.
There's an ancient locomotive
chugging straight across the rug,
getting louder every second . . .
it is probably a bug.

I have counted sheep for hours,
half a million, one by one,
I could have counted walruses,
for all the good it's done.
The alley cats' cacophony
is ringing in my head—
I won't eat ten desserts again
before I go to bed.

## Never Poke Your Uncle with a Fork

Never poke your uncle with a fork,
never kick your uncle in the shins,
never bop your uncle with a cork . . .
these are all unpardonable sins.

If you grab your uncle by the nose,
if you put potatoes on his lap,
if you drop spaghetti on his clothes,
he will make you go and take a nap.

When you're at the table, precious child,
if you start to misbehave, and act
thoroughly undisciplined and wild,
he will gnash his teeth, and that's a fact.

If you jab your uncle with a spoon,
if you prod your uncle with a bone,
you will leave the table very soon,
and have to eat your dinner all alone.

## I Seem to Have a Problem

I seem to have a problem,
I've shrunk to half my height,
my weight has more than doubled,
and my nose is glowing bright.
It's twisted like a pretzel,
I have seven extra eyes,
my ears are like an elephant's,
my feet are giant size.

I knew I was in trouble
when I started growing scales,
and now I've sprouted antlers,
and a dozen fuzzy tails.
My hair has turned to feathers,
and I've got a turkey wattle—
dear genie, I'm so sorry
I released you from that bottle.

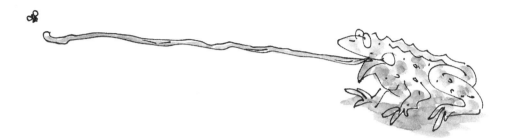

### If I Could Be a Frog

If I could be a frog, then I
would flick my tongue and catch a fly,
and soon without a qualm or thought,
consume the hapless fly I'd caught.

But catching flies is not my plan,
for I'm no mere amphibian.
I am a splendid snake who lies
in wait for frogs who feed on flies.

## Bumble by the Bay

Welcome to the village square
of Bumble by the Bay,
where everyone is strange and rare
from day to day to day.
The mayor kisses sparrows
as he scrubs the judge's nose,
the aldermen chew arrows,
and the sheriff wears no clothes.

The butcher oils the butter,
and the baker bathes the bread,
the florists softly mutter
as they paint the roses red.
The grocer hides tomatoes,
and the doctor juggles clocks,
the barber shaves potatoes,
and the farmers harvest rocks.

The plumbers dress in barrels,
and the masons dress in pails,
the carpenters have quarrels
over who should wash the whales.
It may appear a bit bizarre
to carry on this way,
but that is how the people are
in Bumble by the Bay.

### We Are Plooters

We are Plooters,
we don't care,
we make messes
everywhere,
we strip forests
bare of trees,
we dump garbage
in the seas.

We are Plooters,
we enjoy
finding beauty
to destroy,
we intrude
where creatures thrive,
soon there's little
left alive.

Underwater,
underground,
nothing's safe
when we're around,
we spew poisons
in the air,
we are Plooters,
we don't care.

### I Have a Pet Tomato

I have a pet tomato,
it doesn't have a stem.
My friends have pet asparagus—
why can't I be like them?

## It Is Foolish to Relax

It is foolish to relax
sprawled across the railroad tracks.
You will surely find out why
when the next express rolls by.

### Today Was Not My Day at All

Today was not my day at all,
today was not my day,
for everything went wrong today
in almost every way.
This morning I was menaced
by a troop of marching ants,
I brushed my teeth with shaving cream,
I split my brand-new pants.

I smashed my only glasses,
and the key snapped in the lock,
the toaster didn't toast the toast,
then handed me a shock.
I walked into a doorknob,
something squirmed inside my shoe,
I found an ugly beetle
at the bottom of my stew.

A bird I didn't recognize
flew down and pecked my nose,
a chimpanzee on roller skates
sped by and squashed my toes.
I wonder if I'm under
some unlucky sort of curse,
today's the twelfth, and Thursday—
tomorrow may be worse.

## Snevington Snee

I'm Snevington Snee,
and from seven till three
I hang by my toes
from a coconut tree.

I've plenty of time,
and it's hardly a crime,
and no one seems willing
to do it for me.

## I've Turned into a Carrot

I've turned into a carrot,
it's baffling and strange.
Somehow, while I was sleeping,
I underwent a change.
Last night I was a human,
with head and hands and feet,
this morning I'm a vegetable
I've rarely cared to eat.

I look into the mirror,
and see I'm long and lean.
I have an orange body,
my hair is leafy green.
A further complication
compounds my current woe,
a rabbit is approaching . . .
So long! I've got to go.

# I Gave My Friend a Cuckoo Clock

I gave my friend a cuckoo clock,
he beamed and said, "Sublime!
I love it, love it, love it—
there's no present like the time."

**Zigzag**

SOMETIMES I TAKE A NOTION

.KCAB DNA HTROF GAZGIZ OT

IT TAKES A BIT OF PATIENCE,

.KCANK NIATREC A SEKAT TI

IT'S TOTALLY IMPRACTICAL,

,TIMDA YLIDAER I

TO ZIGZAG VERY FREQUENTLY,

.TI HTIW NUF EVAH I TUB

IF YOU WOULD LIKE TO ZIGZAG,

,WOH NIATRECNU ERA DNA

JUST PAY COMPLETE ATTENTION

.WON GNIDAER ER'UOY TAHW OT

THEN SIMPLY IMITATE IT,

...OD OT EVAH UOY LLA S'TAHT

WITH JUST A LITTLE PRACTICE,

.OOT GAZGIZ LLIW NOOS UOY

## Why Do I Have to Clean My Room?

Why do I have to clean my room
when I would rather play?
The crayons scattered on the floor
are hardly in the way.
I almost never trip upon
my basketball or drums,
and I don't pay attention
to the cake and cookie crumbs.

Why do I have to clean my room?
I think my room looks nice.
There's pizza in the corner,
but it's only half a slice.
I'm not at all concerned about
the gravy on the chair,
my piles of model planes and trains,
my stacks of underwear.

I will admit some bits of clay
are sticking to the wall.
I scarcely even notice them
and do not mind at all.
Beneath my bed there's just a wedge
of last week's apple pie,
and yet I have to clean my room . . .
I simply don't know why.

## I Don't Want To

I don't want to play on the sidewalk.
I don't want to sit on the stoop.
I don't want to lick any ice cream.
I don't want to slurp any soup.
I don't want to listen to music.
I don't want to look at cartoons.
I don't want to read any stories.
I don't want to blow up balloons.

I don't want to dig in the garden.
I don't want to roll on the rug.
I don't want to wrestle the puppy.
I don't want to give you a hug.
I don't want to shoot any baskets.
I don't want to bang on my drum.
I don't want to line up my soldiers.
I don't want to whistle or hum.

I don't want to program my robot.
I don't want to strum my guitar.
I don't want to use my computer.
I don't want to wind up my car.
I don't want to color with crayons.
I don't want to model with clay.
I don't want to stop my not wanting . . .
I'm having that kind of a day.

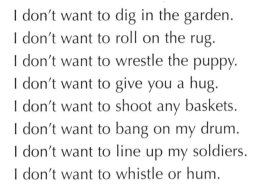

## I Am Shrinking

I am shrinking, I am shrinking,
I am shrinking very fast,
and I'm thinking as I'm shrinking
that this day could be my last.
I don't have a single inkling
why I'm suffering this fate,
Now I'm smaller than a cabbage…
is it something that I ate?

I am shrinking, I am shrinking,
I am dwindling away,
and I hardly need to tell you
this is not a normal day.
Now I'm smaller than a pickle,
than a pencil, than a prune,
and it's patently apparent
I will vanish very soon.

I am shrinking, I am shrinking,
I am smaller than a bean,
and unless there's a reversal,
I will exit from the scene.
I'm receding every second,
now I'm smaller than a flea,
a midge, a mite, a molecule,
and now I'm nothing . . . see?

## There's a Blopp in My Room

There's a Blopp in my room!
There's a Blopp in my room!
I'd better be fetching
a mop and a broom.
To quickly evict a persnickety Blopp,
the trick is to use
both a broom and a mop.

A broom but no mop
is of dubious use,
the Blopp simply giggles,
you feel like a goose.
And likewise a mop
is a flop by itself,
the Blopp merely hops
on the nearest high shelf.

But wielded in tandem,
a broom and a mop
will totally stop
the most obstinate Blopp.
The Blopp will depart,
running fast, going far,
and you will be Bloppless,
as most people are.

## Questions

Can a butcher block and tackle?
May a crossbow tie the knot?
Might a pocket change direction?
Will a talking turkey trot?
Should a station break the ice cream?
Where do balls of fire fly?
Could a clam bake bread and butter?
Does a luncheon counter spy?

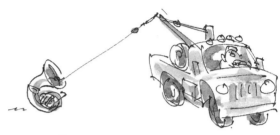

Will a hot dog pound the pavement?
Might a snowshoe tree top spin?
Would a mountain pass the time zone?
May the morning fog horn in?
Should a horse show off its rocker?
Will a sitting duck press pants?
Does a cow shed tears of laughter?
Can a teapot belly dance?

Does a sawtooth pick and shovel?
Should a piggy back away?
May a tow truck stop the music?
Would an egg roll overpay?
Could a light foot hold a candle?
Can a kitchen curtain call?
Might a needle point a finger?
Where does running water fall?

## Waffles Give Me Sniffles

Waffles give me sniffles,
chicken makes me itch,
toffee gives me toothaches,
tacos make me twitch.
Hot dogs give me fevers,
ice cream gives me chills.
If I nibble candy bars,
I'm green around the gills.

Pancakes make me queasy,
spaghetti makes me sneeze.
As soon as I eat pizza,
I get a weird disease.
Peanuts gives me pimples,
popcorn hurts my throat.
One taste of macaroni,
my body starts to bloat.

Raisins give me rashes,
bananas make me shake.
If I bite a burger,
I get a bellyache.
The moment I try chocolate,
I lose a little hair—
broccoli has no effect,
it's thoroughly unfair.

## My Brother Is Totally Bonkers

My brother is totally bonkers,
there isn't a brain in his head.
He heard that it's time for spring cleaning—
he's cleaning the springs in his bed.

## A Piglet

I'm a piglet, pink and stout.
If I'm cold, I sneeze and sniff.
If I have to blow my snout,
I take out my oinkerchief.

## I Am Winding Through a Maze

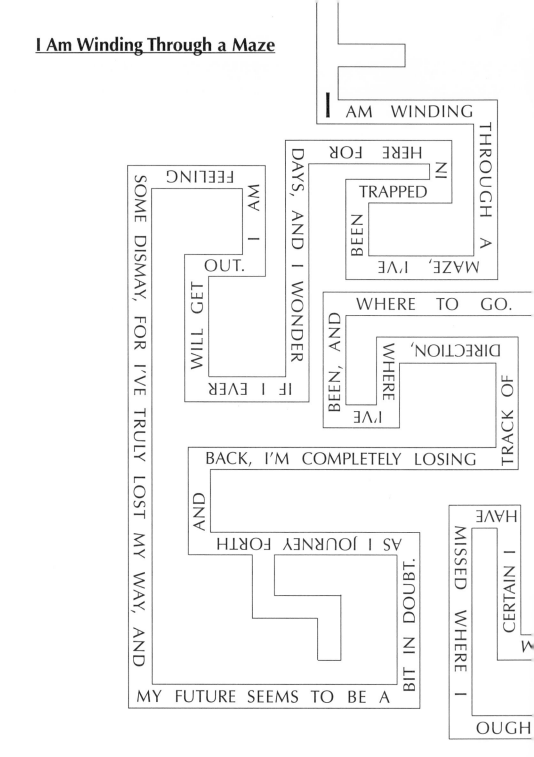

I AM WINDING THROUGH A MAZE, I'VE BEEN TRAPPED IN HERE FOR DAYS, AND I WONDER IF I EVER WILL GET OUT. I AM FEELING SOME DISMAY, FOR I'VE TRULY LOST MY WAY, AND MY FUTURE SEEMS TO BE A BIT IN DOUBT. AS I JOURNEY FORTH AND BACK, I'M COMPLETELY LOSING TRACK OF WHERE I'VE BEEN, AND WHERE TO GO. DIRECTION, I'M CERTAIN I HAVE MISSED WHERE I... OUGH

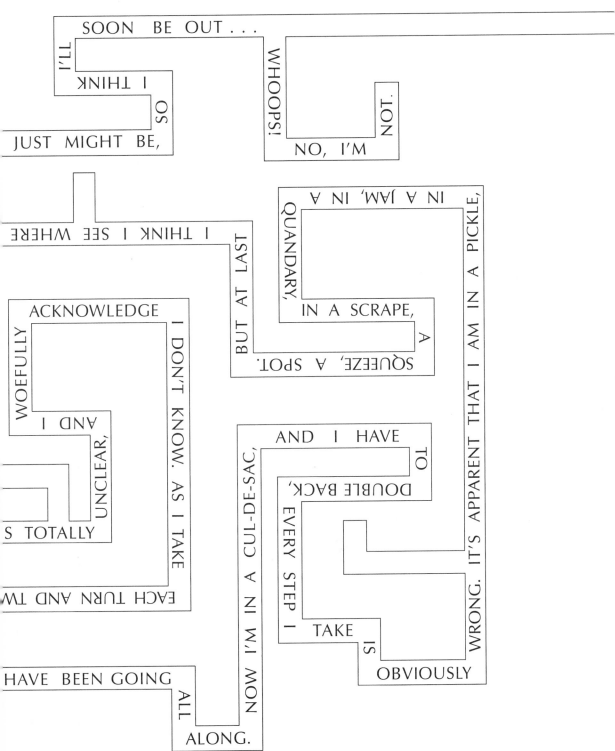

## A Fetching Young Gnu

A fetching young gnu had a penchant for song,
her ringing soprano was thrilling and strong.
Her warbles outclassed the most musical bird,
her trills were the pride of the wildebeest herd.

Her coloratura made jackals rejoice,
hyenas and lions were charmed by her voice.
Her singing grows better with practice and age—
she stars on the Grand Antelopera stage.

## Burp

I have **BURP** a certain habit
that I **BURP** admit appears
to annoy **BURP** many people,
some **BURP** even hold their ears.
I'm not sure **BURP** why I do it,
though it's **BURP** a lot of fun,
but I know that **BURP** at burping,
I am second **BURP** to none.

All my friends **BURP** **BURP** enjoy it
when I **BURP** behave this way,
so I do my best **BURP** burping
any time we **BURP** **BURP** play.
Though I may **BURP** burp a little
when I'm talking **BURP** to you,
be **BURP** very **BURP** **BURP** grateful
that is all I **BURP** **BURP** do.

## I Had an Invisible Playmate

I had an invisible playmate
that nobody else seemed to see,
I doubt they believed it existed,
it showed itself only to me.
Sometimes we chased one another,
sometimes we went for a walk,
sometimes we sat down together
and had a good heart-to-heart talk.

We tossed an invisible beach ball,
we jumped an invisible rope,
we planted invisible flowers,
we climbed an invisible slope.
I thought we'd be playmates forever,
but everything comes to an end—
my grandmother sat on the sofa,
and squashed my invisible friend.

## My Tongue Is Tasting Terrible

My tongue is tasting terrible,
I can't imagine why,
for all I ate was pickled snake,
and chicken beaks on rye.
I had a plate of candied snails,
assorted monkey lips,
a bowl of curdled turtle tails,
a dish of hippo chips.

I tried a bit of weasel cheese,
rhinoceros tofu,
a cup of plankton pudding,
garlic curry kangaroo,
a quart of onion ice cream,
and a slice of walrus pie . . .
my tongue is tasting terrible,
I can't imagine why.

## A Noble Knight-at-Arms

I am a noble knight-at-arms
astride a noble steed,
employed upon a noble quest
to do a noble deed.
Alas, I'm unsuccessful,
though I ride from sun to sun,
my quest goes unrewarded,
and my deed remains undone.

A paragon of chivalry,
I long to do no less
than rescue any rescuable
damsels in distress.
Alack, I'm ineffectual,
I find such damsels late,
and earlier delivered
from an execrable fate.

I ache to tilt at dragons
with my formidable lance,
but swifter knights dispatch them first,
I seem to have no chance.
I hunt for monstrous ogres
to eviscerate, but nay . . .
they prudently absquatulate
while I'm yet well away.

I'm similarly thwarted
at confronting evil trolls,
who sensibly evacuate
their pestilential holes.
Deterred yet undiscouraged,
my resolve is never weak,
though regularly tested
by my singular physique.

But half the height of other knights,
my girth is thrice as great.
My mount is discommoded
by my monumental weight.
At best it barely manages
an apathetic trot.
My name is famed through all the land—
I'm called Sir Lunchalot.

# I'm Building a Bridge of Bananas

I'm building a bridge of bananas,
it's pretty, but not very strong.
Bananas are not very sturdy,
bananas don't last very long.
Initially green, and then yellow,
increasingly speckled with brown,
inevitably, as they ripen,
it's clear that my bridge will fall down.

My bridge is developing fissures
and even some sizable gaps.
It's senseless to try and repair it,
I might as well let it collapse.
It waggles and sags in the middle,
it wobbles and droops at the ends,
and so I've alerted my neighbors,
as well as my family and friends.

They're trucking in freezers of ice cream
of every last flavor that's made,
plus whipped cream and chocolate syrup,
both of a premium grade.
They're bringing me barrels of walnuts,
and cherries without any pits—
we'll shortly be sharing delicious
gigantic banana bridge splits.

## Worm Puree

*W*orm puree, oh hooray!
*You're the dish that makes my day.*
*Sing a merry roundelay.*
*Worm puree, hooray!*

Worm puree, I must say,
you're divine in every way.
Hot or cold, fresh or old,
I'm your devotee.

*Worm puree, oh hooray!*
*You're the dish that makes my day.*
*Sing a merry roundelay.*
*Worm puree, hooray!*

Worms with rice, oh so nice,
every forkful, every slice.
When I chew bits of you,
I'm in paradise.

*Worm puree, oh hooray!*
*You're the dish that makes my day.*
*Sing a merry roundelay.*
*Worm puree, hooray!*

Worms with cheese, mashed with peas,
you are guaranteed to please.
Every bite is delight,
and slides down with ease.

*Worm puree, oh hooray!*
*You're the dish that makes my day.*
*Sing a merry roundelay.*
*Worm puree, hooray!*

Worm puree, pink and gray,
you're a heavenly entree.
Just one spoon makes me swoon,
worm puree, hooray!

*Worm puree, oh hooray!*
*You're the dish that makes my day.*
*Sing a merry roundelay.*
*Worm puree, hooray!*

## A Group of Moose

A group of moose, whose skulls were thick,
attempted some arithmetic.
Of course their efforts were no use,
their minds were but the minds of moose.
Addition was a hopeless act,
and likewise, they could not subtract.
Devoid of acumen and wit,
they could not multiply a bit.

Division was beyond them too,
they clearly did not have a clue.
Percentages just gave them pains,
and fractions overtaxed their brains.
Those addlepated moose were vexed,
uncomprehending, and perplexed.
"We're through with math," they sadly sighed.
"Those numbers have us moostified."

## I'm Fond of Frogs

I'm fond of frogs, and every day
I treat them with affection.
I join them at the **FROG CAFE**—
We love the Croaking Section.

# I'm Ironing My Rhinoceros

I'm ironing my rhinoceros,
removing all the lumps.
I'm smoothing out the wrinkles,
and I'm flattening the bumps.
It takes a lot of trouble,
and it takes a lot of time,
I think it's worth the effort,
for my rhino looks sublime.

The process may be tedious,
but clearly we don't mind,
a wrinkle-free rhinoceros
is very hard to find.
I cover him with polish,
and I buff him to a shine,
there's just one smooth rhinoceros,
and he's entirely mine.

## Hello and Good-Bye

Hello!
I do not think I'm here,
or any other place that's near.
It also seems I am not there . . .
perhaps I am not anywhere.

How can it be that I am not
on this or any other spot?
It doesn't make a lot of sense
and tends to keep me in suspense.

If I'm not here or there, then how
could I be talking to you now,
expecting that you might reply?
It's much too much for me.
Good-bye!

## I'm Being Abducted by Aliens

I'm being abducted by aliens,
and I'm not enjoying the ride.
They simply appeared in their saucer
and beamed me directly inside.
It's creepy and weird in this saucer,
a strange sort of purplish brown,
I can't tell the floor from the ceiling,
in fact, I may be upside down.

The aliens have odd little bodies,
a cross between melons and eggs.
Their hands end in hundreds of tendrils,
they don't seem to have any legs.
They don't seem to have any noses,
they don't seem to have any eyes,
instead, on their heads are medallions
that keep changing color and size.

They're feeding me gloppy concoctions
that taste even worse than they look.
I guess, since they're totally mouthless,
they don't need to know how to cook.
They haven't revealed where we're going,
or why we are taking this tour.
This unannounced alien abduction
is making me feel insecure.

As we hurtle on through the cosmos,
I'm breathing unbreathable air,
yet all my complaints go unheeded,
my alien abductors don't care.
But now I've a pressing dilemma
that simply cannot be ignored,
I'm dying to go to the bathroom—
they don't seem to have one on board.

## There Was Unabated Chaos

There was unabated chaos
in my neighborhood today,
the dogs made awful noises,
and the pigeons flew away.
The neighbors shut their windows
just as quickly as they could,
even traffic took a detour
to avoid my neighborhood.

My parents ran for cover
as they'd never run before,
they ducked into a closet
and abruptly slammed the door.
I sprinted to the country
and I jumped into a creek,
when my brother took the socks off
he'd been wearing for a week.

## A Foolish Cow

A foolish cow, declining greens,
ate jumping and vanilla beans.
Now she quivers, now she quakes,
now she gives vanilla shakes.

## It Was a Sound

It was a sound, an awful sound,
a sound both sharp and flat,
and high and low and screechy,
like the shrieking of a cat.

It was a scratchy scrapy sound,
it sank into my skin,
that sound my sister made today—
she plays the violin.

## I Am Stuck Inside a Seashell

I am stuck inside a seashell, and I don't at all perceive how I got in such a pickle, but I cannot wait to leave. I am winding winding winding through this narrow spiral shape, and I'm sorry that I entered, for it seems there's no escape. I'm in need of extrication, there's no room to turn around, and I'm not the least bit happy, and in fact I'm filled with woe. Won't you point me to the exit? I have nowhere left to go . . .

## Blimmer and Blommer and Blummer and Blime

Blimmer and Blommer and Blummer and Blime
inhabit a clime where it rains all the time.
Not one of the four has a bit of a brain,
or hardly the sense to get out of the rain.

They wander unthinkingly out in the storm,
and never go in where it's cozy and warm.
This dimwitted, blockheaded, clueless quartet
spends every last moment all soggy and wet.

## I Am Cuter than a Button

I am cuter than a button,
I am neater than a pin.
I have freckles on my forehead
and a dimple in my chin.

I have eyes as blue as bluebirds,
I have shiny golden hair,
and a little cherry birthmark—
I will never tell you where.

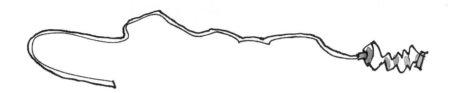

## I'm Standing in the Corner

I'm standing in the corner,
my mom is mad at me,
I'll bet that it's the bubble gum
still stuck to the TV,
or maybe she remembers
that I woke her with my drum,
or could it be the orangeade
in the aquarium?

I wonder if she's angry
that I took apart the phone,
or possibly because of where
she found that ice cream cone.
Maybe it's those vegetables
I hid beneath my bed,
more likely it's a certain word
I accidentally said.

Perhaps I'm being punished
for buttering that bug,
or for the tube of toothpaste
I squeezed out on the rug.
It's probably because I tied
my brother to a tree . . .
I'm standing in the corner,
my mom is mad at me.

## My Brother Shaved His Teddy Bear

My brother shaved his Teddy Bear
about a year ago,
he did a very thorough job
and stripped it, head to toe.
He acted sort of suddenly,
entirely on a whim.
It sounds a bit unusual . . .
it's normal though, for him.

Before my brother shaved it,
it was quite a handsome bear,
but now it looks pathetic
and appears beyond repair.
Its fur was soft and velvety,
luxurious and long.
He thought it would grow back again—
it looks like he was wrong.

## I Went to a Yard Sale

I went to a yard sale
and found it a treat.
They'd run out of yards,
so I purchased three feet.

### Nina Tina Fleener

I'm Nina Tina Fleener,
I'm clean, extremely clean,
I bathe eight times an hour
and shower in between.
I scour my head and shoulders,
my nose and knees and neck,
I rub and scrub so thoroughly,
I never leave a speck.

I wash my ears and elbows,
shampoo my lustrous hair,
I make myself so spotless,
I am beyond compare.
I'm certain not to overlook
my fingers and my toes,
so every single bit of me
splendiferously glows.

When my entire body
is shiny as the sun,
I simply start all over,
my cleaning's never done.
There's just one complication
with staying wet all day—
I'm wrinkled as a raisin,
and I'm shriveling away.

## I'm Glad I'm Not a Firefly

I'm glad I'm not a firefly,
for I suspect I'd mind
a permanent electric light
attached to my behind.

## The Famous Flea Circus

I went to the Famous Flea Circus
to marvel at talented fleas,
there were fleas on minute unicycles,
and fleas on a flying trapeze.
There were fleas turning intricate cartwheels,
while balanced on tightly strung threads,
and fleas climbing poles made of pencils,
while standing on each others' heads.

One was shot out of a cannon
and landed unscathed and intact,
a dozen rode bareback on beetles,
it was a remarkable act.
I loved everything that I saw there
under the tiny striped tent.
Hooray for the Famous Flea Circus—
I'm scratching a lot since I went.

## The Farm's Karate Festival

At the farm's karate festival,
the lambs and mules were tops.
The mules excelled at kicking,
but the lambs had better chops.

## Smedley Smye

Smedley Smye is scared to fly,
he's nervous in the air,
the thought of planes disturbs his brains,
it's more than he can bear.
He starts to cough when he's aloft,
he itches, sweats and groans,
he grits his teeth, he grips his seat,
he shivers in his bones.

He aches, he ails, he bites his nails,
his dinner goes unchewed,
his face turns greener than a bean
when he gains altitude.
He quakes, he throbs, he shakes, he sobs,
his stomach gets upset—
So why oh why is Smedley Smye
the pilot of a jet?

## Dear Wumbledeedumble

Dear Wumbledeedumble, where are you?
You've left without telling me why.
You packed up one night
and you flew out of sight,
without even one bite good-bye.
I'll miss your unnerving appearance,
the wings on the sides of your head,
your feathery chest
and your leathery crest,
the nest that you built in my bed.

I'll miss your assortment of noises,
your whinny, your whistle, your whine,
your single sharp fang,
and the song that you sang
that sent such a chill down my spine.
I'll miss how you started each morning
with some sort of sudden attack.
You munched on my ears
till you drove me to tears.
Sweet creature, oh, won't you come back?

I'll miss your provocative habits,
like constantly chewing my toes,
your deafening howl
and your menacing growl,
the way that you shredded my clothes.
I'll miss your bizarre disposition,
your pungent, unsavory smell,
for now you have flown
and I'm left all alone . . .
dear Wumbledeedumble, farewell!

## Is Traffic Jam Delectable?

Is traffic jam delectable,
does jelly fish in lakes,
does tree bark make a racket,
does the clamor rattle snakes?
Can salmon scale a mountain,
does a belly laugh a lot,
do carpets nap in flower beds
or on an apricot?

Around my handsome bottleneck,
I wear a railroad tie,
my treasure chest puffs up a bit,
I blink my private eye.
I like to use piano keys
to open locks of hair,
then put a pair of brake shoes on
and dance on debonair.

I hold up my electric shorts
with my banana belt,
then sit upon a toadstool
and watch a tuna melt.
I dive into a car pool,
where I take an onion dip,
then stand aboard the tape deck
and sail my penmanship.

I put my dimes in riverbanks
and take a quarterback,
and when I fix a nothing flat,
I use a lumberjack.
I often wave my second hand
to tell the overtime,
before I pick my bull pen up
to write a silly rhyme.

# Index to Titles

# Index to First Lines